Joy in the Journey

CHARLES HOPSON

Printed in the United States of America

Library of Congress Control Number: 2019911638
ISBN: Softcover   978-1-64376-299-9
         Hardcover   978-1-64376-318-7
         eBook   978-1-64376-300-2

Republished by: PageTurner, Press and Media LLC
Publication Date: 08/13/2019

To order copies of this book, contact:

PageTurner, Press and Media
Phone: 1-888-447-9651
order@pageturner.us
www.pageturner.us

A THORN IN THE FLESH

And a knife in my back
Many things I have suffered
This one thing I did not lack

I'm pursued at any cost
To become another martyr
By a seared conscience
From another traitor

I must stand bold
And put on my armor

Draw my sword
And cut to the core

My Father at my side
Is the way I choose
With him as my strength
I cannot lose

ASPIRATION

Searching for traces of hope
Of our divine existence
All thru our far-reaching life
Desiring to make a difference

Wandering in the dark
Void of any light
Thru a murky clouded vision
Blinded by the night

With no where else to turn
Searching for directions
Anxiously seeking out the truth
Left with many questions

Searching for paradise
Seems far beyond our reach

Yet a light at the end of the tunnel
Guiding us thru the breach

No need to look any further
It's closer than you think
In the twinkling of an eye
We are standing on the brink

BACKSIDE OF LIFE

You were lost and confused
With no measure of concern
You continue to search for the truth
Not knowing which way to turn

You spend your days all alone
Searching high and searching low
Then a hand reaches out to you
To show you the way to go

You discover the right path to take
Yet it only last for awhile
You continue to dwell on the past
So you abandon the rigorous trial

You go back too your former life
Feeling the journey is too tough

You fear that you cannot make it
Because you're not strong enough

Just keep your eyes on the Master
Don't worry about all the strife
He will lead you safely home
Away from the Backside of Life

BELIEVE IT OR DON'T

Believe it or don't
The facts do not lie
So just have faith
It will always draw you nigh

It is closer than you can imagine
Of a life that never dies
Continuously thru eternity
From a past that's gone awry

A place of happiness
No more sighs or pain
Just an eternity of joy
Where the Son always reigns

BLACK SHEEP

Of the many shades to choose
You have decided to be black
The color from the dark side
Of the wrong side of the track

You figure that you have no need
Of anyone you can trust
You sense that you are rejected
By the feeling of being unjust

Why do you act the way you do
Rebellious in the way you think
And with no thought of others
As you, continue to sink

You appear to have no conscience
While clothed in shady wool

And with your suspicious ways
You continue to play the fool

In an instant the shade fades
With no need of being in disguise
There can be a change of your color
By showing yourself wise

CELESTIAL DREAM

Filling the imagination
With a picturesque story
Musing all of its splendor
Captivated by all its glory

Envision a sight so beautiful
As a flower blooming in the morn
Opening up to welcome the day
A splendid pleasure to adorn

Acting out all the images
Of thoughts during the night
With a pure, breathe of life
Of an illuminating sight

Could this fascination be true?
Or just another fantasy
As my heart is pounding
With an overwhelming ecstasy

CHANCES SLIM TO NONE

Once there was an effortless way
Of traveling here and there
Yet time has taken a toll
For it seems it does not care

Leaving you uncertain
As your chances begin to decay
Your choices start to diminish
As obstacles hinder your way

Searching for some answers
It reaches the moment of concern
You see your time is running out
Not knowing which way to turn

If you will only look inside yourself
You are sure to find the answer
It has been there from the beginning
For it has been there before you were

COME & GONE

Leaving my place of serenity
On a journey to the unknown
Expectations of the unfamiliar
Fearful feelings of being alone

Where have my travels taken me
Appears to be a place of mystery
Of a region that is full of turmoil
An environment lost in history

A land full of discord and violence
A civilization truly rebellious
Torn asunder by contrasting beliefs
Of a society fully malicious

Sending out an S. O. S
Send Our Savior

COMPROMISE

Why wrestle with the truth
When you have no clue
Of your final fate

Such a dangerous decision
May leave you in doubt
Of your future state

Why jeopardize a just destiny
By being so indecisive
Before it's too late

Don't get yourself sidetracked
Just stay on the right path
Thru the narrow gate

CONDUCTOR

Traversing thru time
Down a one track mind
Aboard a train of thought
Leaving the past behind

A one-way ticket
With no time to rescind
Reimbursement void
Destined to the very end

All-aboard!!!
Now leaving for home
Aperture closing in
Do not get left standing alone

With no stops in between
We are on the express line
The estimated time of arrival
Do not worry it is right on time

CONTEMPLATION

Gazing back at my past
To see where I will be
Looking to my future
Considering what has become of me

Question marks all around
It's tearing me apart inside
I don't know which way to turn
Just cannot find a place to hide

I 'm walking on a tight rope
Without a net below
Seems like the odds are against me
As I try to decide witch way to go

I know there is no time to waste
As my chances are running out
I must make my decision count
Beyond any shadow of a doubt

So if by chance I find a way
To the answer of my plight
I know that I'll never regret
Walking towards the light

Standing at the crossroad
Two ways in which to go
Have to make a decision
From the things we know

Must not make an err
Could jeopardize our fate
Have to make up our mind
There's no time to wait

Only one way that we can go
Need to know where to turn
To soar into the heavens
Or to crash and burn

CUT TO THE CORE

Emotional breakdown
Who is to blame?
Accountability on trial
Time to name names

Who will testify to the fact?
Reveal their status quo
Be a witness to the crime
Confess to what they know

Is there anyone out there?
To stop such a fate
Put an end to this travesty
Before it is too late

If you can reveal the truth
Please step to the fore
Tell us what you've seen
That we can get to the core

DAWN TO DUSK

Conceived into a world
Ensuing upon a new life
Filled with perilous trouble
Of a world plagued with strife

Loosed from our confinement
Liberated from the womb
Set free to wander about
Cast into a life of doom

On a journey full of discord
Destined to fail
Further away from the spirit
Down a hazardous trail

As we come to an end
Our regrets left behind

We face the inevitable
Of a most nullifying kind

Laid in utter darkness
Cascading flume
Of a shallow grave
At the bottom of a tomb

DESOLATE

Low man on the totem pole
The short end of a stick
Candle burning both ends
Quintessential wick

Sitting on the edge
Anticipating every move
The suspense is killing me
With nothing left to prove

Searching for the truth
Patiently waiting for a sign
The closing stages has begun
Hurry it's time to get in line

Stuck in another rut
Going away empty handed
Marked for disaster
Shunned and branded

DILEMMA

Contaminated by default
Mutual tainted disgrace
Common indiscretion
Portraying a two face

An alternative quandary
Feign double minded
Undecided resolution
Selfless twofold blinded

Anonymous mystery
An added enigma
Beyond any doubt
Another dilemma

DISAPPEARING ACT

My special place of refuge
A secret hideaway
Unknown to anyone
Where I plan to stay

You're wasting your time
You'll never find me
Hide and seek
Let it be

Now you see me
Now you don't
Searching for a clue
You know you won't

Erased from life
Better luck next time
See you in the funny papers
If you have the dime

DISCERNMENT

Wide the road that leads to destruction
Narrow the path that leads to life
The choice is up to you

Be careful which way you go
It's the difference between night and day
It could mean the variation on what you do

Depending if you choose to rise to the top
Or if you choose to fall to the bottom
To receive a reward or pay your dues

There's no way of getting around it
Everyone must decide their fate
It's not only up to me it's up to you too

DOWNHEARTED

Reminiscing of times afore
Thru musings of my past
Exposing so ambiguous
Reflecting eras all so vast

Trying hard to see beyond
The things that lye behind
Looking far and looking near
In empty places of my mind

A conscience ever haunting
Convictions that cannot hide
Once locked away in solitude
Now stirring up inside

With the absence of my friend
As my heart grows fonder

Deep affections stirring
With only memories to ponder

Slowly leaving a void
Every moment of the day
As the chasm's getting closer
It is time to kneel and pray

DREAM VACATION

Reflections drifting
Beyond reality
To another realm
A far away tranquility

To a place not known
Of a profound fascination
Fostering subconscious
Shrouded imagination

Lost in a way of thinking
Trapped by my own belief
Searching for a way to escape
From my life of grief

Looking for an opening
In the fabric of time

A celestial stairway
Of which I might climb

Far beyond any vision
A place of true serenity
With all the ones I love
Throughout eternity

DREW A BLANK

My mind appears to be confused
Concentration at a loss
Wandering around in a fog
Thoughts separated like the dross

How can I regain my senses
Flood my head with more muse
Get myself back on track
Discover all of the right clues

Pondering all of these inclinations
I stand all alone totally confused
Looking deep into my reflection
Trying to discern why I was defused

ELEVEN FIFTY NINE

The sand of time has shifted
Bringing an end to all grace
The aperture is closing in
With an end to the human race

And as the curtain falls
There seems to be no doubt
We are standing on the brink
As our time is running out

We must make a decision
As to avoid any strife
Where do we want to be
Concerning the after life

There is one thing for sure
With no need to mention
We must make a choice
Staying here is no option

So make up your mind
Before it is too late
Everything depends on
Sealing your fate

EMOTIONAL AWAKENING

Feelings stirring up inside
Many emotions are revived
Restoring thoughts of the past
Dead memories have come alive

What could cause such a rouse
To allow them to be set free
And to essentially run amuck
With an uninhibited spree

With entire senses preoccupied
Clouding up the imagination
Leaving no room for doubt
Apart from a minds-eye sensation

They must be brought under control
Gathered together as one

Captured and rounded up
To put an end to their madcap run

I have put my past behind me
With the renewing of my mind
There will be no more interfering
With all the things I left behind

EMOTIONAL ROLLER COASTER

Full of it's ups and downs
With indecisive dealings
Caught in a quandary
Of separating feelings

What is a person to do
When you must make a choice
Do we flip a coin to see
Or listen to the still small voice

I don't claim to be a rocket scientist
Yet I do know one thing for certain
When the play comes to an end
It will bring down the final curtain

Who will be there at the close
To accept at the end of days
The appreciation due
And receive the final praise

EMPATHY

Reflections in a looking glass
Like shadows in the dark
Window gazing in the rain
Silently walking in the park

No one there to notice us
Staring thru obscured eyes
Waiting hopelessly to be seen
From a world that cannot cry

Do you feel the sorrow
Or take time to be heard
With a seared conscience
Stepping over fallen words

Do you need an invitation
Written especially just for you

Before you will act in response
Or have you even a clue

Premeditated thought well planned
Of another empty notion
Spontaneous reaction from the heart
Already set in motion

ENDURANCE

Tricks of sundry kinds
Intentions to deceive
Hidden from prying eyes
If that's what you believe

The ocean wave's farewell
Sand castles melting away
With the sounds of fainting sighs
As the quick sand devours its prey

Facing a quandary
Trapped in the spiders web
Snared by slothfulness
As our years quickly ebb

Do not be confused
There's always a solution

Many a way to escape
With a final resolution

Look past the circumstances
To see what there is to see
Of a solid alternative
Beyond all human expectancy

ENUFF Z NUFF

Standing on the edge
Reached my breaking point
Time to turn things around

Make a change for the best
Focus all my intentions
From being lost to being found

Setting my sights on faith
Of the straight and narrow
Path that is heaven bound

Avoid any and all distractions
Listening for the shepherd's call
For we all know that familiar sound

ESCAPE FROM PARADISE

Running to nowhere
Down ancient ways
Searching for a reason
Thru forgotten days

Going around in circles
Past similar places
Catching a glimpse
Of unfamiliar faces

Try to make sense of it all
Yet I still haven't got a clue
As the world continues spinning
Confusion clouding my every view

I know I must get back home
For that is my destiny
To the place I left behind
To be with all of my family

EVERLASTING DEVOTION

What can I say?
I have been captivated
Charmed beyond belief
And truly fascinated

Thoughts overwhelming
Of an alluring charm
Of love and splendor
Which go arm in arm

Could I sense other feelings?
As my emotions, escalate
If there was any other way
I know now that it's too late

I know that I have gone too far
To the other side of the track
I have crossed over the fine line
Now there is no turning back

I would not have it any other way

EVERY PICTURE TELLS A STORY

Standing all alone in a crowd
Who could imagine as much
To be a part of an ordeal
Or to play a role as such

With no uncertainty to the matter
For it is the way it was meant
A missing part of the assembly
As everyone came and went

Reading between the lines
Will leave you nowhere
Caught in a state of animation
While you stand and stare

Just another senseless moral
Without any type of epilogue

No beginning or any ending
As we're left standing in the fog

Speechless without a tale to tell
Lost for words to say
As the portrait begins to fade
At the light of day

FALLEN

Looking up and looking down
In the midst of total confusion
Reality no longer exist
Leaving an empty conclusion

With nowhere left to turn
You realize there's no way out
With thoughts slowly fading
They leave you in doubt

Try to make sense of it all
Searching for true reality
Seems to be lost in time
With a sense of mediocrity

A righteous man may fall seven times
Yet he will always make a stand
For everything that is for the good
Being there to lend a helping hand

FATHERS FAVORITE

Who is the Fathers favorite?
The one in whom he loves the best
And the one he watches over
The person who is daily blest

I sincerely believe
To him we're all priceless
He loves everyone just the same
And our time with him will be ageless

For our love for him
Is beyond all measure
We could never place a value
Even if we had the worlds treasure

FAUX SINCERITY

Empty promises
Of lies that bind
Self deception
Of devious kinds

Who do you think your fooling
With your pack of lies
You better think twice
Straighten up and get wise

Look around and you will find
It's not that easy to deceive
The one who is omniscient
For now is the time to believe

With the insight to see
Of a spiritual nature
Forsaking the past
Pursuing all things pure

FINAL CHAPTER

So many episodes in the past
Of a life of mystery
Doesn't seem to be a plot
In this small part of history

Searching for a meaning
A tiny clue to the story
Some idea of the concept
Revealing all of it's glory

Cannot wait for the epilogue
For the final conclusion
To find out how it all ends
Will it be real or an illusion

FIRST IMPRESSION

Am I a reflection in my mind
Or perhaps a translucent hologram
A mirage image of myself
Another predetermined program

I look to the mirror for an answer
Can I truly believe everything I see
So many times I have been deceived
It's hard to know If I am to be or not to be

A vacant doppelganger in disguise
With two sides to every tale
One on the right the other on the left
The difference between heads or tails

If I only knew what I was talking about
Perhaps I could see the reality
Or at least be somewhat close
With a chance at mediocrity

FRAYED

Our time is running out
As the end is drawing near
It was finished at the cross
Therefore, I have nothing to fear

The bad times have vanished
Buried in memories of the past
Leaving my soul tattered
From years that never last

From all the crooked trails
That I have ever traveled
Everything I have ever done
Has left my life unraveled

Time for a little stitch in time
With a renewal of my mind
Renew the things that remain
By leaving the past behind

FURTHER MORE

Glitch in time
Stymied for a moment
Drew a blank
Of an intention spent

Things happen
Sometimes for the best
Yet not for me
I have not time to rest

With so much to say
I have to keep going
No time to quit
My intentions are showing

With my feelings exposed
Of my deepest aspirations

And my senses revealing
My overwhelming sensation

I must suppress my bygone thoughts
Bury them far down deep
Never again to be awakened
Leaving them to an eternal sleep

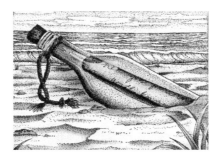

FUTURE REFERENCE

A victim of my own device
Slave of my own misdealing
Captive of an empty life
Heart void of feeling

Freedom in which to choose
Desire to follow my own will
Prerogative to live my own way
My impending future to fulfill

Intricate part of a fallen race
A world that's been deceived

By a source that's unreliable
They too had once believed

Reached the end of the road
In my passé glory
Termination achieved
Epilogue to the story

GLASS MENAGERIE

Messages in a Bottle
Afloat on the sea of dreams
Filled with tear soaked letters
Crying out their forgotten themes

Drifting on an endless current
Caught by the binding tide
Just like a vanishing mirage
As all their hopes have died

And with no land within sight
Without, any hope of reaching shore
They seem to be lost forever
And to never return no more

Lost out in the ocean
Stillness all so fair
Motionless tranquility
Thru the night time air

GUIDANCE

Premeditated plans
Are well thought out
Spontaneous reactions
May leave many doubts

Spiritual guidance needed
Leading us alongside
Our escort and our shepherd
Our companion and our guide

Along the narrow path
To the Lords kingdom
For anyone that is willing
For everyone is welcome
Heavenly Blessing

How could I ever find another?
More beautiful than the one I love
Of a vision so exquisite
Sent down from above

Could this simply be a dream?
I pinch myself to see if it is real
As I realize that, I am not asleep
I am aware of the emotions I feel

My life shall never be the same
For that, I am forever thankful
You fill in me an empty void
Therefore, I am eternally grateful

I find it all so hard to believe
Of a personage so caressing
My passion is overwhelmed
Of a divine Heavenly Blessing

HIDDEN TREASURE

Spending a lifetime searching
For something that's been lost
You exhaust all your resources
For whatever the cost

Digging for the truth
Cannot seem to locate a trace
All hope is suddenly diminishing
It seems the past has been erased

` What is next on the agenda?
Seeking help from a higher source

Choose an alternative solution
By following a diverted course

The answer to the dilemma
Is to look for some assistance
For today is the day
To seal your eternal existence

HOLLOW SHADOWS

Stalking unsuspecting souls
In which to devour
As the day fades
Hour after hour

Lookng for refuge
Somewhere to stall
Hide and seek
Behind the wall

Here today
Gone tomorrow
Vanishing act
Alluding sorrow

HOPE IN THE JOURNEY

With a seared conscience
Singed around the edge
Leaving a burnt state of mind
Another stringent dredge

Looking for the meaning of it all
It's just a prayer away
Your search will not be in vain
It is as clear as the light of day

When things seem the darkest
With all traces becoming weak
And the eyes become blinded
Never give up to seek

Many things hidden from sight
Although they can be discovered
By searching out the truth
You find they can be uncovered

ILLUSION

Now you see them
And now you don't
All the things you could
And the things you won't

As the mystery unfolds
Before your very eyes
Only there for a moment
Until they pass you by

The some of matters long-ago
Things that never meant to be
Without any intention to exist
Which in time eventually flee?

Images disappear without a trace
Like shadows in the night
Mirages quickly vanishing
Swept away by the light

KNOW YOUR ENEMY

As we travel thru this land
Not everyone we meet is our friend
There are some that wish us harm
With no willing hand to lend

We must always be watchful
By using our spirit of discernment
Distinguishing the fiery arrows
Of which the enemy has sent

Putting on the full armor of God
Given to us for protection
That the victory shall be the Lord's
By the divine intervention

LEAVING FOR HOME

Feels as if I've spent an eternity here
How long, there's no real telling
Though nothing will be missed
Of this temporary dwelling

Time for me too move on

With no coming back
As I reach the point of no return
To the other side of the track

Content sitting on the porch
Of my Fathers house back home
Leaving all of my past behind
Never again to ever roam

LONG TIME NO SEE

It's been such a long time
Since we have been together
So tell me how have you been

I have certainly missed you
It just hasn't been the same
I'm so glad we can be together again

Welcome home my friend
Please won't you come inside
That we might get reacquainted

And to reminisce of our past
Of our never ending friendship
An endless love that is true hearted

MAKING TRACKS

A long road well traveled
Going nowhere in particular
Headed for a place in time
Of a destination unfamiliar

Searching for a new dwelling
Anywhere that I can call home
Drifting along like the wind
Stirring across the loam

Traversing down thru time
Seeking one place or another
Towards the ends of the earth
For a place unlike any other

Where my journey will lead me
As I hit the dusty trail
I do not have the foggiest idea
Going over hill and over dale

MANIFESTATION

Written on the winds of time
Plainly visible to the eye
Illuminating the darkness
As the final hour draws nigh

The truth lies in the balance
The weights are placed upon the scale
With no denying the accuracy
As the evidence will plainly tell

Proof of the matter must be known
For you cannot dispute the truth
Once the verdict has been handed down
The sentence cannot retract

MARGIN OF ERROR

Seems to good to be true
The thoughts of perfection
In a world full of mistakes
With no concept of correction

Yet who can know the difference
Is anyone capable of such a task
And able to unveiling the mask
By revealing the absolute truth

Punctuations standing in the way
Blinding the meaning of it all
Separating fiction from reality
Leaving a society subject to a fall

MEMORABLE

Time is getting short
So they say
We might not have
Another day

So I'm returning
To a prior place of yore
Many familiar surroundings
Been here before

Great to be home

MIND-SET

Premeditated plans
Well thought out
A temporary delay
No doubt

Many deeds undone
Attempting to hide
Tomorrow is another day
Your tasks set aside

Good deeds undeserving
Meaningless to the King
Leave them behind
They don't mean a thing

Sincerity is faithfulness
To go beyond and above
Directly from the heart
Of an unspoken love

MISPLACED

Colors fading from the picture
Seems to have lost it's hue
Perhaps missing in time
Without leaving a clue

Another disappearing act
Vanishing in thin air
Did it actually exist
Was it really there

Only time will tell
There's a mystery to it
From the very soul down
To the everlasting spirit

MONOTONY

Fjord echoing crash
Lost without a trace
Fading images
Emotionally erased

Point of no return
Dead end walking
Senseless dialogue
Irrational talking

Many words written
Imprisoned rages
Vacant inane letters
Filling empty pages

Ideas eradicated
Purposes banished
Empty canvas fading
Shadows vanished

NAYSAYER

Sometimes a question arises
Leaving much to think about
Throwing caution to the wind
So when in doubt toss it out

Problematic solution unhidden
We must see with eyes to see
Unscrambling the parable
It's as plain as you and me

No need to think twice
The answer is so apparent

While staring you down
It's the way it was meant

To seek out the truth
As easy as one, two, three
When it all adds up
The sum is what it should be

NEW BEGINNING

Now you see it
And now you don't
Disappearing from view

Once it was visible
Then it vanished
As away it flew

Searching can result
In leaving avoid
Without a clue

Looking for something
That doesn't exist
What is there to do

One thing for certain
Nothing last forever
As all things become new

NEW WORLD ORDER

Pentagon or pentagram
Dimensional symbol
The all seeing eye
Watching in limbo

Have the masons
Paid their dues
Local union confederacy
Leaving many clues

Denial of a secret pledge
Members forever bound
Hidden from the truth
Made when no one's around

Concealed from society
Of a faction that surpasses
Slipping thru the cracks
Unnoticed by the masses

NIGHT SHADOWS

Empty dark and clouded room
Shadows dancing across the floor
Dust seeping from an empty crypt
Sifting sunlight thru an open door

Searching for a little consolation
Solace on a crowded sphere
A place for me to hide away
Escaping from all of my fears

A radiance softly exposing
Secrets carefully locked away
Broken key in a rusted lock
Sealed from the light of day

Enigma of the darkness
Veiled from prying light
Buried deep in mystery
In shadows of the night

NO DEPOSIT & NO RETURN

Looking near - looking far
Searching high - searching low
Escaping from a captive past
From the clutches of the foe

Gazing over the shoulder
Seeking a glimpse to find
Was I there along the way
Or just a moment in my mind

Looking back to where I am
Imagine what I used to be
Ahead to see where I have been
Clearing a way that I might see

Thoughts are my only friend
Staring at pictures of home

Reminiscing of life that was
In the gallery beneath the loam

One more sidetracked diversion
Another one way sojourn
Counterfeit direction misleading
With no deposit and no return

NO SECOND CHANCE

It's all been said before
That he who hesitates is lost
With no where to be found
You may as well count the cost

You see there is no bargaining
And you won't find a loophole
For you see it is inevitable
For the redeeming of the soul

The choice is up to you
To choose the right direction
At the second coming
Of the final resurrection

So don't be fooled by no one
Predicting insignificant signs
For you know there is only one
Who really knows the end of times

NOT A DRY EYE

The tears of a clown
When no one's around
The silence never broken
As the laughter dies down

Sitting all alone
No solitary pleasure
Amusement runs out
Empty of any measure

The cheers become still
No one to show admiration
All alone in our thoughts
Void of any appreciation

NOWHERE TO BE FOUND

Reminiscing of times afore
Thru musing of my past
Exposing so ambiguous
Reflecting eras all so vast

Trying hard to see beyond
The things that lye behind
Looking far and looking near
In empty places of my mind

A conscience ever haunting
Convictions that cannot hide
Once locked away in solitude
Now stirring up inside

With the absence of my friend
As my heart grows fonder

Deep affections are awakening
With only memories to ponder

Slowly leaving an empty void
Every moment of the day
The chasm is getting closer
Devouring everything in it's way

OH WELL

Drinking water from the well
Satisfying an essential thirst
Only with a momentary desire

The cistern has finally dried up
As all the contents have evaporated
Leaving nothing but the muck and mire

Yet there is a source that will never end
Which the giver of life will always supply
And your faith is all that is required

Never again drinking from an empty cup

OUTCASTS

Looked upon as peculiar
Different from all others
Appearing uncommon
Indifferent to one another

Shunned by a majority
Cast out from the crowd
Banned from association
From the separated proud

Yet saved from the world
Bought with a price
Redeemed by the shepherd
The living sacrifice

PERCEPTION

Premeditated plans
Are always well thought out
Spontaneous reactions
May leave you in doubt

Every good discernment
Is spiritually selective
Leaning toward understanding
For wisdom is perceptive

Cannot rely on intuition
The truth is the only way
For discovering the certainty
As plain as night and day

PERSEVERE

Simple deception
Tricks of the trade
Seen nothing new
As the years fade

You say you've seen it all
And that you are strong
That nothing is impossible
That you cannot go wrong

Be sure that you're on coarse
Don't get lost along the way
Keep looking straight ahead
You haven't the time to stray

You try to block it out
Yet it's still there

With no place to go
Remember to beware

Don't get shut in
It's time to get out
Before it's locked away
Without a doubt

PREDESTINED

Chosen from the beginning
To arrive at my destination
No two ways about it
There's no time for consideration

I've been invited to come home
To be with my the ones I love
With no second guessing
I'm headed to my dwelling above

No time to look back
My last deed has been done
I just cannot wait no longer
The journey has already begun

PRETENSE

Concealing the truth
Veiled barricade
Theatrical satyr
Cleaver masquerade

Counterfeit deception
Deceitful disguise
Twofold impression
An overshadowing demise

Obscure charlatan
Death mask depiction
Transparent identity
Deceiving inscription

Snake oil peddler
Nickels of wood
Disappearing act
Your words are no good

Stow away
In your hide-out
Secret places
No-doubt

Sign pointing the way
Seek and go find
Years fade to grey
Don't get left behind

PUNCTUATION

Inserted into the lines
Added declaration marks
Causes to allow so many
To be left out in the dark

Comma sense appended
What could it mean
When taken out of context
What else is there to be seen

Misunderstood meaning
Mistaken identification
Adversely incorporated
Unjustified contradiction

So don't believe everything
Of appended punctuations
They may not always be
Of a precise interpretation

QUEST

Traveling to nowhere in particular
Just another spontaneous whim
Searching for much brighter days
And escaping a past so grim

An existence of a vivid array
The essence of a placid life
To live free of any discord
Completely void of any strife

A journey to the very end
By staying on track
Reached the end of the line
With no turning back

Realizing that I have arrived
I'm finished wandering around
For there is no place like home
Where familiar surroundings abound

RACE FOR TIME

Traversing down thru time
Across familiar ground
Moving faster and faster
Predestination bound

Face to face with my adversary
To settle things left undone
Running in the race for time
The showdown has begun

Round and about I go
The world about me a blur
Could I be on the right path
I cannot say for sure

Heading for life's end
My final destination
Thru an open door
My special invitation

RAGS TO RICHES

From the wrong side of the tracks
Lacking prominent hue
Born without a silver spoon
With a total different value

Ignored by an eminent society
Blinded by self-esteem
Out of focus perception
For all the world to deem

Vision hidden from their view
By the glint and glamour
Nearsighted to a fault
An appearance of a snake charmer

REALITY

A Novel Idea

Slips in when we're not looking
Leaving us in a quandary
We don't like what we see
Of the way it invades our boundary

So we engage our defense
Setting up our force shield
As we make it very hard
For the opposition to yield

Is there anyway to escape
Such a fatal circumstance
Can we make a run for it
Do we even have a chance

There is one thing I know for sure
The time for such an endeavor
Has left us with a small window
Of opportunity for now or never

RECOVER

Looking up and looking down
In the midst of total confusion
Reality no longer exist
Leaving an empty conclusion

With nowhere left to turn
As we emotionally go round
Spinning effortlessly
We are nowhere to be found

Try to make sense of it all
Searching for true reality
Seems to be lost in time
With a quality of mediocrity

A righteous man may fall seven times
Yet he will always attempt to arise
For he knows for certain
How to reverse his demise

REDEMPTION

You have stolen my heart away
Something I thought I could hide
I will no longer be the same
With feelings stirring up deep inside

Destined to walk the earth
As someone completely anew
An existence of a novel life
With a totally different hue

Although it's unfamiliar to me
As emotions souring upon a wing
And my feelings being overwhelmed
I would never change a thing

I did not see it coming
As it caught me by surprise
One thing it has taught me though
It's difficult to cover up a disguise

REMINISCING

Pictures of home
Filling my mind
Missing my family
Of an agape kind

As I sit weeping
Tears flowing from my eyes
Reminiscing of the past
Longing for my time to rise

If I could have one wish
I know what it would be
Just to be back home
Amongst my family

Father I Miss You

RESTORATION

Fallen words
Never spoken
Deafened sound
A promise broken

Disappointed vow
Trust ridden astray
True faith shattered
Unraveled and frayed

Fellowship torn asunder
For by a moment in time
Everlasting forgiveness
For repentance of the crime

Time healing all wounds
Restoring broken hearts
Reconciling differences
With a brand new start

Wandering thru life
In search for the truth
Down many rabbit trails
Nothing seems to be foolproof

Highway to Heaven
Highway to hell
Road to nowhere
Who can tell

Sidetracked in my thinking
Flip a coin to choose
Heads I'm a winner
Tails I lose

There must be a better way
Of deciding my destiny

I fall to my knees
With an earnest plea

As I look to the heavens
I bow and I pray
I truly need to know
Of the truth and the way

ROUND ABOUT

Imprisoned by my rival
In a circular bastille
Leaving me with no way out
My chances of escaping nil

Sealed within a hollow
With no means to getaway

Pacing in my round about
Forever to be kept at bay

Trapped inside an empty sphere
Entombed for an epoch duration
Cannot see the light of day
Facing eternal damnation

RUNNING OUT OF TIME

With all hope diminishing
Short term in the distance
Forefront in short supply
Disappearing at a glance

Just another dead end
Unavoidable circumstance
Fixed terminating closure
Without a second chance

My future in question
Inescapable stance
Illuminating future
Brilliantly enhanced

And with no where to turn
I've finished my last dance
For it time I was on my way
And so I must advance

SANITY CLAUSE

Searching for a loophole
Tiny opening to slip thru
Another easy way out
Waiting for your queue

There's no time to turn about
Must go with the flow
For the time has come to pay
The compensation owed

Another familiar Déjà vu
You know it's not a dream
Perhaps another nightmare
A terrifying theme

Trying hard not to believe
Seems to good to be true
More than just a fairytale
What are you going to do

Excuses just won't get it
With the elders of yore
You're just wasting your time
It has all been tried before

May as well surrender
As not to be forsook
To ignore all the signs
Is to be overlooked

SECOND TO NONE

Running in the rat race
I seem to be far from first
I have a lot of catching up to do
Before it starts getting worse

Yet in my race for home
Although I gave my all to run
I knew everyone would be a winner
For the prize has already been won

Long ago when a tomb was sealed
It was thought that it was done
Yet when the stone was rolled away
That's when the quest for home begun

All the chosen were tied for first
So there was no second to none
As we reached the finish line
We were welcomed by the Fathers Son

SEEKING THE TRUTH

Traces of hope
Divine point of view
Profiting many
If you only knew

Blinded by the light
Left out in the dark
Forsaken by many
Missing the mark

No where to turn
Identity in question
Seeking the truth
Cautionary mention

Searching for paradise
Far beyond your reach

Light at the end of the tunnel
Traversing the breach

No need to look any further
It's closer than you think
In the twinkling of an eye
Your right on the brink

SERVING OTHERS

A trustworthy friend
Never counting the cost
Always sharing what he has
For the sake of the lost

Never second guessing
Nor taking time to pause
Freely giving-not expecting
Anything for the cause

A friend will always be there
When things are looking bleak
Interceding for the forsaken
A defender of the weak

SHADOW OF A DOUBT

Shrouded in mystery
Skepticism aloof
A veiled silhouette
Concealing the truth

Thoroughly disclosed
Hidden from prying eyes
Buried in secret places
Cloaked in disguise

If your looking for a clue
It's just another regret
You won't find it anywhere
And that's a sure bet

SHADY OUTLOOK

Always playing the fool
By listening to lies
Not using my discernment
To show myself wise

Ego swollen pride
Another sure bet
Blinded third eye
That's what I get

Joker running wild
Leading me astray
Why am I so naive
By believing what may

Time span variation
So very plain to see
Why can't I perceive
And to let it be

Caught between a rock and a hard place

SHELL OF A MAN

As I muse over my regret
Of the substance of my past
I was unaware of the matter
Not realizing it would never last

For the essence of the time
I was truly naive
Lost in a meaningless moment
And vulnerable to deceive

Though the years have taught me
Over a tiring elongated span
That I would eventually become
Just another shell of a man

SHORT SIGHTED

Can't win for losing
Try as hard as I may
So grateful for bad luck
Just to make it thru the day

If it wasn't for bad luck
I would have no luck at all
Just caught in limbo
Another victim of the fall

Seem to be the low man
Always looking up
Vision short sighted
At the bottom of an empty cup

SHORTCUT TO NOWHERE

Another forsaken realm
With no place left to run
Tried to take the easy way
Yet I'm back where I begun

Where do I go from here
As I end up at the beginning
I thought there was a reason
Now I find there is no meaning

Just another outcast all alone
Back at the finish line
Leaving me with no way out
As my chances continue to decline

Looking over the big picture
I see I took a wrong turn
Time to get on the right track
And accept a lesson learned

SHOW US THE WAY

Lead the way
Through the hallow
Point the way
And I will follow

Out for a walk
No need for a sign
Stay close to the leader
Along the strait line

Walking along
The road leading home
Don't turn about
There's no time to roam

Before you know it
Your standing at the door
Welcomed home with open arms
Of the one you've been waiting for

SILENT PARTNER

Unknown to so many
Familiar to the one he loves
A good and faithful servant
Going far beyond and above

Unseen by the multitude
Yet always in the Master sight
Aware of everything he does
A friend for his master's plight

Absent from the lime light
No center of attention
A presence not made known
Of a name rarely mentioned

Always willing to serve
At a moments notice
Void of any hesitation
Negated of any malice

Goodman of the house

SINK OR SWIM

How long can you tread water
By keeping your head afloat
For the odds are against you

With no place to swim
Bobbing up and down like a cork
You find your time is thru

And with no where else to turn
Your time is running out
As your chances have been too

Now's the time to seek some help
From the one with a lending hand
That you might start anew

SOUL SEARCHING

Seems I have always been
On the short end of a stick
A candle burning at both ends
Just a quintessential wick

Sitting on the edge
Anticipating every move
The suspense is killing me
With nothing left to prove

Searching for the truth
With selfless anticipation
Patiently waiting for a sign
Some kind of indication

Stuck in another rut
Going away empty handed
Marked for disaster
Shunned and branded

SOW WHAT

An epoch old question
Past down thru the ages
Troubling many for years
All thru the history pages

There must be an answer
To such a mystifying theme
Yet who knows the truth
To the confounding deem

We all know the difference
Between right and wrong
And with the help from above
We have the strength to be strong

If we wish to make it back home
We must follow a strait row
So to accomplish our goals
And to reap the benefits we sow

SOWN TO REAP

A crushing sorrow
Of a shattered kind
Sad and broken
Effects that bind

You must pay the fiddler
If you choose to dance
With no recompense
And no second chance

Stuck in a rut
Narrow and deep
With no way out
Sown to reap

STEPPING OUT

Skipping rocks across a pond
That only sink to the bottom
Never too be seen again
Disappearing just like Sodom

As we step out in the faith
Leaving our doubts behind
We continue on our quest
Of an enthusiast kind

Using our spirit of discernment
Being careful not to be deceived
For all things are possible
For everyone that believes

SUBMIT

Soulful recommended use
Before the expiration date
To ignore the warning
May cause a serious fate

Nothing last forever
You need not pretend
It is said that all good things
Eventually come to an end

To not know better
Is not to attempt to try
Not to seek out the truth
Is the remedy to die

To be vindicated
Is to fully surrender
Not to submit thyself
Is to fall asunder

SUPPRESSED

Ability from the beginning
Stored carefully within
Subconsciously unaware

Secrets hidden away
Inspirational feelings
Deep within the lair

If I had only known
I could have revealed
Just how much I care

Only one thing it would take
To bring it to the surface
Was the confidence to share

THE END

All good things
Must come to an end
For nothing last forever

We try to hang onto
All material of the past
With all our might to endeavor

Yet at some point in time
We must accept the fact
That it is time to render

And so when we realize
That the moment has arrived
All we can do is to surrender

THE TRUE MEANING OF IT ALL

Who will supply the answer
Is there anyone that knows
If so please step forward
Before it all comes to a close

Time seems to be running out
As the light is fading away
Our moment has come to an end
We may not have another day

What will we find when it's over
Of the existence on the other side
Will we just be a memory
Or have a place to abide

THRESHOLD

Searching for traces of hope
Of our divine existence
All thru our far-reaching life
Desiring to make a difference

Wandering in the dark
Void of any light
Thru a murky clouded vision
Blinded by the night

With no where else to turn
Searching for directions

Anxiously seeking out the truth
Left with many questions

Searching for paradise
Seems far beyond our reach
Yet a light at the end of the tunnel
Guiding us thru the breach

No need to look any further
It's closer than you think
In the twinkling of an eye
We're right there on the brink

TILL WE MEET AGAIN

Long time no see
How long has it been
It seems like forever

Separated for a moment
Thou it feels like an eternity
When will we be together

Counting the moments
Waiting to return home
Days seem to be getting longer

If I ever needed patience
I know that I need it now
For the hope to make me stronger

Yet I will never give up
In the promise that you made
Of our fervor for one another

TIME SHARE

Who's counting the years
As they quickly fly by
And the difference of space
That's between you and I

Who's keeping track of it all
Of the things that should never be
Or who is the keeper of the fall
And the watchman holding the key

Time waits for no one
For it cannot stand still
Moving ahead before our eyes
Progressing at will

Before you know it
It's a whisper in the breeze

A long time forgotten
Just like memories that flee

Seasons may come
And seasons may go
Yet when it's all said and done
Who will actually know

TODAY'S, TOMORROWS YESTERDAY

Here today
Gone tomorrow
Seek & find

Unlike any other
No way typical
One of a kind

Similar to none
A solitary time
Momentary blind

Yet nearer than before
In a minds eye
Close behind

TODAY'S, YESTERDAYS TOMORROW

Forgotten memories
Lost in time
Vanished

Here for a moment
Just a split second
Banished

Scarcely momentary
A fading mirage
Diminished

Though when it's all over
We will soon be there
Finished

TOWARDS THE FUTURE

I've left the past behind
All that amounted to nothing
My memories have been erased

Cannot see behind my present
Everything that I knew
Has now been misplaced

No longer to be revealed
The pictures of the lost
Have now been defaced

Removed from all existence
Like shadows in the night
Never leaving any trace

TRANSFORMATION

We are born completely physical
Yet our spirit it was not
For it must be awakened
Thru a sacrifice to be bought

We are born without an awareness
Of a reason virtually unclear
And the existence of our life
Of the meaning why we are here

While seeking out an answer
To the meaning of it all
We stumble upon an epiphany
Of a much higher call

It beckons us to search the truth
That we may find the purpose

Of the true meaning of our life
With a trinity so truly wondrous

For he who began a good work in you
Will carry it on until it is done
Unto the day of the Lord
For the battle has been won

TRAVERSING TIME

Traveling to nowhere in particular
Just another spontaneous whim
Searching for much brighter days
And escaping a past so grim

An existence of a vivid array
The essence of a serene life
To live free of any discord
Completely void of any strife

A journey to the very end
By staying on track
Reaching the end of the line
With no turning back

Welcome to your new home
Built just for you in mind
With three boards and two nails
Of the most compassionate kind

TRAVESTY

Concealing the truth
Veiled barricade
Theatrical satyr
Cleaver masquerade

Counterfeit deception
Deceitful disguise
Twofold impression
An overshadowing demise

Obscure charlatan
Death mask depiction
Transparent identity
Deceiving inscription

Snake oil peddler
Nickels of wood
Disappearing act
As if you could

Stow away
In your hide-out
Secret places
No-doubt

Sign pointing the way
Seek and go find
As years fade away
Don't get left behind

TRUST

A word lost in time
Where did it go?
Could it be hiding
Does anyone know

I would like to find out
As it was a one of a kind
When all else would fail
It was a friend of mine

At times it is hard to meet
Anyone you can believe
Does anybody take notice
Or have we all been deceived

Searching for the truth
For one who could truly care
Of a divine intervention
With a sincere love to share

TRUTH OR CONSEQUENCES

Staring into a looking glass
At a parallel reflection
Of things I don't want to see
Leaving an negative reaction

Although it reveals the saying
Fool me once shame on you
Fool me twice shame on me
I'm left short of any clue

Will I take heed to all of this
I suppose that only time will tell
If I allow my wits to let it be
Shrouded behind my veil

So to put an end to all of this
And, learn a valuable lesson
I must set the iniquitous free
By ignoring any dissension

Looking ahead
Clouded pretension
Two way thoroughfare
In either direction

Only one way out
The choice is up to you
Decide carefully
May be the last thing you do

Take a closer glimpse
For seeing is believing
One road leading to the dead
The other to the living

Wide the gate leading to destruction
Freeway
Strait the gate leading to life
Pathway

UNVEILING

Searching the very soul
Exposing secrets gone astray
When seeking out the truth
Don't get lost along the way

Numerous created situations
Forgotten and left behind
Nothing that is spontaneous
Only of a premeditated kind
Who let the cat out of the bag
To be pursued by the pack
For curiosity killed the cat
Yet satisfaction brought it back

Seeking out yet not finding out
Looking here and looking there
Searching high and searching low
With a closer gaze and a further glare

VANISHED

Thoughts left behind
Clouding my view
No place left to go
Nothing left to do

Empty and void
Space in time
Eternally vacant
Epitomized paradigm

Remembering nothing
Reckless contemplation
Meaningless attribute
Flashback imagination

Cannot think clearly
Vague point of view
Confusion all about
Without a clue

VANISHING POINT

Where has the time gone
It was here a moment ago
I only turned away for a second
Where it has gone I don't know

Time it waits for no one
As sand thru an hourglass
Although we continue to beckon
It just seems to pass

We are just a mere mirage
Wavering off in the distance
No matter how much we believe
It disappears in an instance

There is nothing we can do
Too change the inevitable
Except to envisage to reckon
For it is not irreversible

VANITY

A member of society
You try to look your best
Adorned in the latest fashion
You stand-up above the rest

Looking in a different direction
The parade passes you by
As you are left all alone
You consider the reason why

Searching to find an answer
For the lack of concern
You discover that your demise
Is the price of a lesson learned

By reaching out to find the truth
You find what you were looking for
It's always been closer than you think
Of where you haven't looked before

VANQUISH

Worthy of the cause
With a passionate desire
Initiating straightway
A source that is so dire

Advance without hesitation
Swiftly running headlong
There is no turning back
Time to be forcefully strong

Radiant heavenly reflection
An aura of the trinity
Pure principles and morals
Echoing true divinity

Reflected picture image
Of a trusted friend
Closer than a brother
Till the dying end

VESTIGE

Clouded memories
Insight a fading hue
Evidence out of reach
Disappearing from view

Looking for an answer
A response has passed you by
Returning to your lair
With a disappointed sigh

Like skipping rocks
Across a shallow pool
Do you have any clue
Or have you been fooled

Seeking out the truth
Searching for the light
It's closer than you think
Hidden in plain sight

VISIONS OF HOPE

Visions of hope
Divine point of view
Profiting many
If only you knew

Left out in the dark
Hidden from the light
Forsaken by so many
Wondering thru the night

No where to turn too
Identity in question
Seeking out the truth
With sincere intension

Searching for paradise
Far beyond your reach

Light at the end of the tunnel
Traversing thru the breach

No need to look any further
It's closer than you think
In the twinkling of an eye
Your standing on the brink

WALK ABOUT

Going out into all the world
With something important to say
Bringing hope to everyone
Of an answer to knowing the way

I found a resolution to our end
Of unlocking the door to infinity
The entrance into a new life
By the master with the key

Spoken of by the prophets of old
Of the one who would set us free
Paying the price that we owed
By giving his own life on a tree

If we will only accept his sacrifice
The gift of his self that he offered
And have total faith in the day
Of which he died and suffered

And putting all our sincere faith
In leaving behind any regret
Than we can spend eternity with
The one that paid our debt

WALK ON WATER

Nothing will be impossible
When you ask and believe
If you have faith without doubt
Then you shall receive

Every gift that is given
Is a blessing from above
Reigning down from heaven
Soaring on the wings of a dove

If we have faith as a mustard seed
Along with a spoken respond

We can then move mountains
Like skipping rocks across a pond

Tides that bind capture waves
For it is plain to sea
Then we can walk on water
As we command the winds to flee

WALK THE PLANK

Passengers wanted
Plenty of room
So don't hesitate

See the world
Or what's left of it
Before it's too late

Deal of a lifetime
Come aboard
Seal your fate

If you're running behind
Do not worry
They are sure to wait

But if you're not sure
That it is the right day
Then check the date

For if you miss the boat
You are not alone
Just a second mate

WALKING THE TIGHT ROPE

A dubious decision
Loosing your sight
You fall to the left
Or fall to the right

You hit rock bottom
No place left to go
Fallen thru the cracks
It's the ultimate low

Time to make a choice
Of which side of the fence
You would rather land
And spend an era hence

Time to rise up
Make a grave decision
Dust yourself off
Stop following an illusions

WHEN YOU GOING TO WAKE UP

Seems that you haven't learned
Anything from your past
When you going to wake up
Search for the things that last

You've been fooled more than once
It's time you opened your eyes
Take a real good look around
At all of your life in disguise

You know much better than that
For this is not your first time
So don't go and get tripped up
And return to the scene of the crime

Always remember the gospel truth
By relying on your discernment
Then you will make the right decision
And save yourself from internment

WHERE ARE WE NOW

All good things
Eventually come to an end
For time waits for no one
As the years, descend

They never hang around
They go by us too and fro
Now you see them, now you don't
As moments come and go

They seem to disappear
Right before you're very eyes
When you least expect it
It will be the final demise

WHO AM I

As I try to recall my past
I don't remember very much
It appears to be a total blur
It certainly does seem as much

If my life was to flash
Before my very eyes
I would need a rerun
With me the time just flies

Looking back I get lost
I cannot recall a whole lot
As my thoughts are scattered
Like a mystifying plot

I try to imagine where I was
It seems so difficult to see
Staring into a two way mirror
Reflecting the other side of me

WHO KNOWS

I had a thought once
It got lost and I cannot find it
Where did it go

I search the recesses of my mind
It's nowhere to be found
With no results to show

How things suddenly disappear
Now you see it and now you don't
I guess you reap what you sow

I know one thing for sure
It's harder to go up stream
Than to go with the flow

Who'll Figure

CPSIA information can be obtained
at www.ICGtesting.com
Printed in the USA
LVHW052123160919
631219LV00008B/229/P

9 781643 763187